ITALIAN TRACTION

Andrew Cole

AMBERLEY

First published 2017

Amberley Publishing
The Hill, Stroud
Gloucestershire, GL5 4EP

www.amberley-books.com

Copyright © Andrew Cole, 2017

The right of Andrew Cole to be identified as
the Author of this work has been asserted in
accordance with the Copyrights, Designs and
Patents Act 1988.

ISBN 978 1 4456 6646 4 (print)
ISBN 978 1 4456 6647 1 (ebook)

British Library Cataloguing in Publication Data.
A catalogue record for this book is available from
the British Library.

Origination by Amberley Publishing.
Printed in the UK.

Introduction

Italy has had a long association with railways, with the first line opening in 1839. The country built up a large network of lines during the nineteenth century and this extended into the twentieth century, when the first high-speed line was completed just before the Second World War.

The railways in Italy are still state-owned, and are called FS (Ferrovie Dello Stato). There are two subsidiaries of FS: RFI (Rete Ferroviaria Italiana), who look after the infrastructure, and Trenitalia, who run the majority of the trains. There are also a small number of privately run railways, who mainly rely upon multiple units for their services.

Trenitalia run both passenger and freight services, but the freight services now come under the name Mercitalia.

On the passenger side, services are split between four various degrees of service, with the slow services coming under the Regional banner. These services are in the hands of Class 464 locomotives, and also various Minuetto units, as well as Class 425 Jazz units.

The next level is the Regionale Veloce, which are fast regional services, with these mainly being in the hands of Class 464 locomotives. There are over 700 of these locomotives in service and they can be found the length and breadth of the country.

After that is the Inter-City level of service, which is operated by Class 444 and Class 402 electric locomotives. The Class 402s are currently being rebuilt as single-cab locomotives, and will be renumbered into Class 401s. The Class 444 locomotives date from the 1960s and are currently being stored as they are replaced.

The highest level of service are the Freccia (Arrow) services, which use the high-speed lines, again with different levels, from Frecciabianca, to Frecciargento, with the highest level being the Frecciarossa services.

There are still plenty of electrically operated freight workings, with the majority being in the hands of the Class 652 locomotives, but the unusual Class 655/656 articulated locomotives still also appear in abundance. The Class 633 locomotives are slowly being stored and withdrawn, while the early Class 424s and Class 646s are being withdrawn totally.

Italy is an unusual network in mainland Europe in that its overhead electric lines run on 3,000 V DC. The wires on the high-speed lines run on 25 kV AC.

On the diesel side there are not too many passenger services operated by diesel locomotives, with just small pockets in the country, including the line to Siena, using the large Class D445 locos.

RFI have a large fleet of diesel shunter locomotives that are based at the majority of stations, which are easily identifiable as they are painted yellow, and originated in various parts of Europe before finding their way to Italy.

This album is not intended to be a thorough, detailed history of the railways of Italy, rather more of a snapshot of the current operations in the country. All in all there is plenty of variety to see and travel on in Italy, and it is a very friendly country to visit. The scenery and history are second to none, and I can fully recommend visiting the country, which is often neglected by enthusiasts. I hope you enjoy looking through my collection of modern photos of Italy.

NTV No. 09, 28 March 2017

NTV No. 09 rests at Salerno having arrived with a terminating service. These high-speed units are privately owned, and are operated by NTV (Nuovo Transporto Viaggiatori) under the italo brand.

NTV No. 14, 27 March 2017

NTV No. 14 departs Roma Tiburtina while heading towards Roma Termini. There are twenty-five of these highly impressive Alstom-built units in service. They comprise eleven cars, with varying degrees of comfort.

CLF No. 25, 30 March 2017

CLF No. 25 is seen in the engineering sidings at Livorno Centrale. This shunter is operated by CLF (Costruzioni Linee Ferroviarie), Bologna. There are many small private shunters based in Italy, mainly coming second-hand from other countries in Europe, and CLF No. 25 was formerly No. 7103 in the Belgian NMBS/SNCB fleet.

RFI No. 0092, 31 March 2017

RFI No. 0092 is seen stabled at Orte, just outside of Rome. This small shunter was originally in the Swedish SJ fleet as their V4 No. 149, hence the large 'V4' on the cabside. Almost every medium-sized station in Italy has one of these departmental shunters based there.

RFI No. 0219, 30 March 2017

RFI No. 0219 is seen stabled just outside Firenze Santa Maria Novella station. This shunter was formerly TI No. 214 4032 when it was in the main Trenitalia fleet, and is now operated by RFI (Rete Ferroviaria Italiana), who are responsible for the infrastructure of the Italian railways.

EAV No. 126 509, 28 March 2017

EAV No. 126 509 is seen at Napoli Centrale. This three-car unit was built in 1991 by Firema and is operated by EAV (Ente Autonomo Volturno), being used on local commuter trains around Naples.

DISPO No. 189 402, 27 March 2017

DISPO No. 189 402 passes through Roma Tiburtina with a rake of Cargowaggons. This loco is from the large Siemens-built Euro Sprinter class of locomotives. This particular locomotive is owned by Dispolok, and is one of a handful that regularly work in Italy. This loco also carries the number ES 64 F4-402.

CFI No. 190 322, 29 March 2017

CFI No. 190 322 is seen passing through Ancona with a rake of Cargowaggons. This locomotive is operated by CFI (Compagnia Ferroviaria Italiana), and is one of two Siemens-built Taurus locomotives in their fleet.

CFI No. 191 012, 29 March 2017

CFI No. 191 012 is seen at Terni while shunting a rake of Cargowaggons. This Siemens-built Vectron is one of just two in the CFI fleet. There are not too many Vectron locomotives operating in Italy when compared to other countries in Europe.

TI No. 214 4279, 29 March 2017

TI No. 214 4279 is seen at Ancona. This small shunter is seen stabled among some condemned stock, but has received its new UIC number of 98 83 2214 579-4. It still retains its FS cast number plates with its FS number on them.

TI No. 220 025, 29 March 2017

TI No. 220 025 is seen departing from Ancona. This three-car DMU was built by PESA, Poland, and carries Regional livery, complete with Swing logos. The official number for this unit is ATR 220 Tr 025. There are forty of these units in use with Trenitalia.

GTT No. 234 001, 1 August 2016

GTT No. 234 001 is seen arriving at Torino Lingotto. This four-car EMU is operated by GTT (Gruppo Torinese Transporti), and they operate local services in the Turin area. This class of unit is similar to the Trenitalia Class 425 Jazz unit, and they are part of the Alstom Coradia Meridian family.

EAV No. 243 204, 28 March 2017

EAV No. 243 204 is seen at Napoli Centrale. This two-car EMU was built by Firema in 2014 and is one of nine such units in the EAV (Ente Autonomo Volturno) fleet.

TN No. 245 001, 13 October 2015

TN No. 245 001 is seen at Milano Centrale. This unit is operated by Trenord and is used on the Malpensa Aeroporto route. There are fourteen of these Alstom Coradia units in use, and at the time they carried different advertising liveries, but have since reverted to carrying Malpensa Express livery.

TI No. 245 2177 and No. 464 554, 29 March 2017

TI No. 245 2177 is seen hauling TI No. 464 554 through Foligno station. Foligno is the location for one of the main electric locomotive workshops, and the Class 464 loco has just been released following repairs inside the works.

TI No. 245 2218, 30 March 2017

TI No. 245 2218 is seen stabled at Livorno Centrale. This 0-6-0 shunter was one of 186 Class 245/21 locomotives built from 1976 onwards. This also carries a new UIC number of 98 83 2245 380-2.

TI No. 245 2270, 1 August 2016

TI No. 245 2270 is seen on station pilot duty at Torino Porta Nuova. This shunter is seen coupled to a rake of overnight sleeper carriages. Italy still has many pilot locomotives found working at stations and yards throughout the country.

TI No. 245 6074, 29 March 2017

TI No. 245 6074 is seen waiting for the signal at Foligno station. Of note on this shunter is the adaptor coupling fitted to allow it to couple to Class 464 locomotives.

RFI No. 270 026, 28 March 2017

RFI No. 270 026 is seen at Napoli Centrale while engaged on infrastructure work. This locomotive is a former DB Railways Kof-built loco, and was numbered 333 681 in the German DB fleet. It is now operated by Ferone Pietro, but also carries an RFI number.

RFI No. 270 105, 27 March 2017

RFI No. 270 105 is seen stabled at Roma Tuscolana, awaiting its next turn of duty. This locomotive was built in 1973 for Plasser Italiana as their T5722.

RFI No. 270 113, 2 August 2016

RFI No. 270 113 is seen at Genova Piazza Principe while engaged on infrastructure duty. This was being used to shunt new paving stones for the platform while resurfacing work was being carried out. This is former German DB Kof-built locomotive No. 332 103 that has moved to Italy.

RFI No. 270 157, 2 August 2016

RFI No. 270 157 is seen stabled at Genova Nervi. There are numerous examples of departmental shunters to be found all over Italy, many coming from different European countries. Information is hard to find on their origins, this 0-4-0 being an example whose origin I'm not too sure of.

RFI No. 270 185, 28 March 2017

RFI No. 270 185 stands awaiting its next turn of duty at Formia-Gaeta. This locomotive was formerly in the FS fleet of shunters, being a Class 225.6 locomotive.

RFI No. 270 391 and No. 270 392, 30 March 2017

RFI No. 270 391 and No.270 392 stand coupled together at Livorno Centrale. These locomotives appear to be rebuilt former Czech-built Class 740 locomotives, but information is again hard to find on their true origins.

TPER No. 350 009, 2 August 2016

TPER No. 350 009 is seen arriving at Milano Rogoredo with a service to Bologna. There are twelve of these five-car units in use with TPER (Transporto Passeggeri Emilia Romagna), which were built in 2009 by Stadler of Switzerland.

TPER No. 350 102

TPER No. 350 102 stands at Milano Centrale carrying the attractive TPER livery. The ETR 350.1 class of units is the second batch of Stadler-built 'Flirt' EMUs ordered by TPER, and they were introduced from 2014 onwards. There are just seven of them in use.

TI No. 400 01, 27 March 2017

TI No. 400 01 is seen powering through Settebagni with a high-speed working. There are fifty of these units in service and they were built by AnsaldoBreda, which became part of Hitachi from 2013 onwards.

TI No. 400 10 and NTV No. 13, 28 March 2017

TI No. 400 10 and NTV No. 13 are seen side by side at Roma Termini. The Class ETR 400 unit is operated by Trenitalia, whereas the Class ETR 575 alongside is privately owned by NTV. These two units represent the highest levels of travel on the Italian network at present.

TI No. 400 18, 27 March 2017

TI No. 400 18 departs from Roma Tiburtina with a high-speed working. These units are finished in Frecciarossa red livery, and are branded as the Frecciarossa 1000 trains.

TI No. 400 20, 2 August 2016

TI No. 400 20 is seen on the buffer stops at Milano Centrale, having arrived with a high-speed Frecciarossa 1000 working. The majority of major stations in the main cities in Italy are terminus stations, rather than through stations.

TI No. 400 25, 28 March 2017

TI No. 400 25 is seen stabled in the high-speed carriage sidings just outside Napoli Centrale. It is seen alongside classmates TI No. 400 28 and TI No. 400 30. There are fifty of these eight-car units in service.

TI No. 400 34, 28 March 2017

TI No. 400 34 is seen at Napoli Centrale having arrived with a Frecciarossa 1000 working from Salerno. These units are the newest of the high-speed electric units in service with Trenitalia.

TI No. 402 017, 27 March 2017

TI No. 402 017 is seen at Roma Termini, having arrived with a terminating Inter-City working. There are forty of these electric locomotives in use with Trenitalia and they are used mainly on Inter-City passenger workings, as well as on overnight services.

TI No. 402 018, 13 October 2015

TI No. 402 018 passes through Milano Rogoredo, being hauled towards Milano Centrale. The forty members of this class are known as the Class 402a as there are two different types of Class 402 locomotives.

TI No. 402 025, 2 August 2016

TI No. 402 025 heads through Milano Rogoredo, heading for Milano Centrale. This class dates from the mid-1990s, and was built by Ansaldo Transporti. There are five prototypes that have been withdrawn from service, leaving forty production examples in service.

TI No. 402 031, 28 March 2017

TI 402 031 is seen arriving at Roma Termini with a rake of overnight sleeper carriages. This class of locomotives is used on Inter-City workings, as well as on the overnight sleeper trains, sharing the duties with the Class 402b locomotives.

TI No. 402 033, 27 March 2017

TI No. 402 033 is seen working straight through Roma Tiburtina with an Inter-City working. The Class 402a locomotives are currently being refurbished by CAF, and the work will include the removal of one cab, leaving just a single-cabbed locomotive.

TI No. 402 034, 8 October 2014

TI No. 402 034 is seen stabled at Milano Centrale, awaiting its next turn of duty. The look of these locomotives will change dramatically when they are rebuilt with just a single cab.

TI No. 402 036, 8 October 2014

TI No. 402 036 works an Inter-City service through Milano Rogoredo while heading for Milano Centrale. The majority of Italian locomotives, and indeed electric units, carry two pantographs.

TI No. 402 045, 29 March 2017

TI No. 402 045 stands on the buffer stops at Roma Termini, having arrived with a terminating Inter-City service. This is the final member of the forty-five-strong class, although the first five prototypes have been withdrawn.

TI No. 402 102, 2 August 2016

TI No. 402 102 is seen arriving at Genova Piazza Principe with a Thello passenger working. This locomotive would uncouple after arriving at the station, and a Class 444 loco took the working on.

TI No. 402 103, 1 August 2016

TI No. 402 103 is seen on the buffer stops at Torino Porto Nuova. This locomotive carries Frecciabianca livery, with small branding applied. The Class 402b locomotives are an upgraded development of the Class 402a locomotives.

TI 402 106, 31 March 2017

TI No. 402 106 departs from Roma Tiburtina while carrying unbranded Frecciabianca livery. The Class 402b locomotives are used mainly on Inter-City and also Frecciabianca passenger workings throughout the country.

TI No. 402 112, 2 August 2016

TI No. 402 112 is seen at Milano Centrale, having arrived with a terminating Frecciabianca working. The loco carries small Frecciabianca logos on the bodyside. Frecciabianca translates as 'white arrow'.

TI No. 402 118, 2 August 2016

TI No. 402 118 is seen stabled on one of the centre roads at Genova Piazza Principe. The Class 402b locomotives differ from the Class 402a locomotives in that they can also run on the 25 kV AC high-speed lines, as well as the traditional 3,000 V DC lines.

TI No. 402 120, 28 March 2017

TI No. 402 120 is seen arriving at Salerno with an Inter-City working. This class of locomotives carry the two different liveries for the different services, with TI No. 402 120 carrying Trenitalia livery. Despite this, Trenitalia-liveried locos can still appear on Frecciabianca workings, and vice versa.

TI No. 402 124, 13 October 2015

TI No. 402 124 is seen waiting for departure time at Milano Centrale. This loco carries Frecciabianca livery, complete with two logos on the bodyside, and also has a matching rake of single-deck carriages attached.

TI No. 402 126, 13 October 2015

TIO No. 402 126 is seen at Milano Centrale carrying Frecciabianca livery. The loco is coupled to a rake of Thello-liveried coaches, while working a Milan to Marseille working. Thello was set up as a joint venture between Transdev and Trenitalia.

TI No. 402 137, 13 October 2015

TI No. 402 137 stands on the buffer stops at Milano Centrale, having arrived with a Frecciabianca working. This view shows the awkward positioning of the running numbers on Italian locomotives, on the front bufferbeam. They also carry UIC numbers on the bodyside and cast number plates.

TI No. 402 159, 8 October 2014

TI No. 402 159 is seen stabled at Milano Centrale, awaiting its next turn of duty. This view clearly shows the UIC number halfway along the bottom of the bodyside, and also the cast number plate underneath the driver's window on the far cab. TI No. 402 159 is one of twenty Class 402b locos equipped to run under the French 1.5 kV DC lines.

TI No. 402 165, 8 October 2014

TI No. 402 165 arrives at Milano Centrale with one of the former signal boxes in the foreground. There are two of these impressive structures at the station.

TI No. 402 166, 27 March 2017

TI No. 402 166 arrives at Roma Tiburtina with an Inter-City working. This locomotive carries Frecciabianca livery, as well as a large logo on the bodyside. These locos are also used on overnight services in Italy.

TI No. 402 172, 8 October 2014

TI No. 402 172 is seen on the buffer stops at Milano Centrale. This view shows more clearly the large Frecciabianca logo applied to some members of this class. The train consists of a rake of matching stock.

TI No. 402 173, 28 March 2017

TI No. 402 173 is seen making a station call at Salerno while carrying Trenitalia livery. The loco is at the head of an Inter-City working that is heading towards Napoli Centrale.

TI No. 402 180, 27 March 2017

TI No. 402 180 powers north through Settebagni station while carrying Frecciabianca livery. The next major station on this line is Orte, where the line to Ancona splits from the line to Florence.

TI No. 403 001, 1 August 2016

TI No. 403 001 is seen at Torino Porta Nuova, having hauled a rake of overnight sleeper carriages into the station. There are twenty-four of these locomotives in use with Trenitalia, all carrying Trenitalia livery.

TI No. 403 002, 2 August 2016

TI No. 403 002 arrives at Genova Piazza Principe with an Inter-City working. This view shows the improved positioning of the running number on this class of locomotive. These locomotives were built by AnsaldoBreda from 2006 onwards.

TI No. 403 020, 1 August 2016

TI No. 403 020 is seen having arrived at Torino Porta Nuova with an Inter-City working. Originally these locomotives were intended for express freight workings on the high-speed lines, but all are now operated by the passenger division. They were also able to work under the French 1.5 kV DC lines, but this equipment has since been removed.

RFI No. 404 502, 13 October 2015

RFI No. 404 502 speeds through Treviglio station. This is one of two Class ETR 404 sets that have been taken over by RFI. This particular set is painted in yellow and blue livery, and carries Dia.Man.Te lettering on the side.

RFI No. 404 538, 13 October 2015

RFI No. 404 538 speeds through Treviglio on a high-speed test working. This is the other power car in the Dia.Man. Te test set. These are conventional power cars that have been taken over by RFI to test the electrical equipment on the high-speed lines.

TI No. 404 602, 8 October 2014

TI No. 404 602 speeds through Milano Rogoredo with a Frecciarossa high-speed working. Until the introduction of the ETR 400 Class units, these trains were the pinnacle of high-speed travel in Italy.

TI No. 404 610, 28 March 2017

TI No. 404 610 is seen on the buffer stops at Napoli Centrale. These trains operate in up to twelve-car formations with a power car at either end. The power cars are interchangeable, but tend to stay in fixed formation. The number '28-B' on the front relates to the rake of carriages, and has nothing to do with the power car, although the car at the other end will have '28-A' on the front.

TI No. 404 625, 29 March 2017

TI No. 404 625 is seen making a station call at Ancona while working a Milano Centrale to Bari Frecciarossa working. Frecciarossa translates as 'red arrow'.

TI No. 404 647, 31 March 2017

TI No. 404 647 is seen at Roma Tiburtina. This class of power cars is highly impressive with their matching carriages, and is the backbone of the Italian high-speed operations.

TI No. 404 656, 30 March 2017

TI No. 404 656 is seen having just departed Firenze Rifredi station and is just moments away from Firenze Santa Maria Novella, the main station in Florence. These power cars were built by TREVI in two batches from 1999 onwards, with the Class ETR 404.6 cars dating from 2004.

MIR No. 405 009, 29 March 2017

MIR No. 405 009 is seen making a call at Ancona for a crew change. This batch of forty-two locomotives was originally intended for Polish operator PKP, but they were bought by Trenitalia.

MIR No. 405 036, 29 March 2017

MIR No. 405 036 is seen stabled at Terni, awaiting its next turn of duty. Terni is located on the line between Orte and Foligno. The locomotives in this class have recently had their UIC lettering changed from Trenitalia to Mercitalia.

TI No. 414 100, 8 October 2014

TI No. 414 100 passes through Milano Certosa on the back of a Frecciabianca working. Sixty of these power cars were built by TREVI in 1996, and were rebuilt by Bombardier ten years later.

TI No. 414 102, 1 August 2016

TI No. 414 102 stands at Torino Porta Nuova with a Frecciabianca working. These power cars work the same as the Class ETR 404 cars, in that they are interchangeable between rakes of coaches.

TI No. 414 123, 29 March 2017

TI No. 414 123 passes through Falconara Marittima while heading for Ancona. This station is right on the Adriatic coast, and the sea can be seen in the background.

TI No. 414 124, 1 August 2016

TI No. 414 124 rests on the buffer stops at Milano Centrale. All sixty power cars in this class wear Frecciabianca livery.

TI No. 414 136, 29 March 2017

TI No. 414 136 is seen arriving at Ancona with a Frecciabianca working. These locomotives usually operate around the north of the country.

TI No. 414 159, 2 August 2016

TI No. 414 159 is seen passing through Milano Rogoredo with a Frecciabianca working. These workings have a power car at either end of the train.

TI No. 424 306, 29 March 2017

TI No. 424 306 is seen condemned at Ancona. This class of locomotive dates from the mid-1940s and all have now been withdrawn from traffic. Over 150 locomotives were built by various different manufacturers.

TI No. 425 019, 1 August 2016

TI No. 425 019 is seen departing Torino Lingotto with a local working. EMUs of this class are known as Jazz units, hence the branding underneath the first passenger window.

TN No. 425 032, 13 October 2015

TN No. 425 032 is seen at Milano Centrale. This unit is one of a batch operated by Trenord, based in Lombardy. The ETR 425 Class of unit were built by Alstom from 2014 onwards.

TI No. 425 041, 27 March 2017

TI No. 425 041 is seen approaching Roma Tuscolana. This unit carries Leonardo Express livery, and is one of a small batch allocated to Roma for working non-stop between Roma Termini and Fiumicino Airport.

TN No. 425 059, 8 October 2014

TN No. 425 059 is seen arriving at Milano Certosa while on a test run. This unit had yet to enter traffic at this time. Of note is the first class section in yellow.

TN No. 425 064, 2 August 2016

TN No. 425 064 is seen on the buffer stops at Milano Centrale. There are now over 100 of these five-car articulated units in use in various pockets all over the country.

TI No. 425 101, 29 March 2017

TI No. 425 101 is seen stabled in the sidings adjacent to Orte station. The livery carried by these units is very pleasing to the eye.

TN No. 426 007, 8 October 2014

TN No. 426 007 is seen making a station call at Milano Certosa. This four-car EMU carries Trenord livery, and is one of just nine allocated to the Lombardy region.

TI No. 426 049, 27 March 2017

TI No. 426 049 is seen making a station call at Settebagni. This four-car unit carries Trenitalia green and white livery, but this is gradually being phased out in favour of the new grey and blue livery.

FS No. 428 202, 27 March 2017

FS No. 428 202 is seen being hauled through Roma Tiburtina. There were nearly 250 of these locomotives built from 1934 onwards, and all were taken out of traffic by 1988. They run on an unusual 2-Bo-Bo-2 wheel arrangement.

TI No. 444 011, 8 October 2014

TI 444 011 is seen passing through Milano Rogoredo. This class of locomotives dates from the mid-1960s and was built for Inter-City workings, which it is still employed on today.

TI No. 444 019 and TI No. 444 005, 1 August 2016

TI No. 444 019 and TI No. 444 005 are seen coupled to an Inter-City working at Milano Centrale. This class of locomotive was rebuilt in the late 1980s/early 1990s, and as a result had new angled cabs fitted.

TI No. 444 040, 1 August 2016

TI No. 444 040 is seen departing Torino Lingotto with an Inter-City working. This class is slowly being withdrawn, as the locomotives are approaching fifty years of age. Of note is the class number of the front of the loco: E.444R, the 'R' indicating that it has been rebuilt.

TI No. 444 046, 2 August 2016

TI No. 444 046 is seen stabled on one of the centre roads at Genova Piazza Principe. These locomotives are used on Inter-City workings, as well as express services.

TI No. 444 048, 1 August 2016

TI No. 444 048 is seen on the buffer stops at Torino Porta Nuova station, having brought a rake of Trenitalia-liveried single-deck carriages into the platform. A Frecciabianca-liveried Class 402b locomotive can be seen alongside.

TI No. 444 053, 29 March 2017

TI No. 444 053 speeds through Falconara Marittima with an eight-coach Inter-City working heading for Ancona. The Adriatic Sea can be seen in the background.

TI No. 444 066, 2 August 2016

TI No. 444 066 is seen passing through Genova Nervi with an Inter-City working. This is a beautiful little station, right on the Ligurian Sea, and is complete with palm trees.

TI 444 089, 8 October 2014

TI No. 444 089 is seen approaching Milano Rogoredo while hauling a rake of Frecciabianca-liveried single-deck carriages, complete with a driving trailer right behind the locomotive.

TI No. 463 006, 30 March 2017

TI No. 463 006 makes the station call at Livorno Centrale with a Frecciabianca working. This Class ETR 463 nine-car EMU carries set number 26, and there are there are currently nine of them in service.

TI No. 463 007, 2 August 2016

TI No. 463 007 is seen arriving at Genova Brignole with a Frecciabianca working. This train also has its own set number, with this car carrying set number 27A, while the car at the other end carries set number 27B.

TI No. 463 058, 2 August 2016

TI No. 463 058 passes straight through Genova Nervi while heading for Genova Piazza Principe. The Ligurian Sea can be seen as the backdrop to this scene.

TN No. 464 015, 8 October 2014

TN No. 464 015 is seen departing from Milano Certosa with a Trenord passenger working. This class of locomotive totals over 700 examples in the Italian fleets, which are today the most numerous main line electric locomotives in use in the country.

TI No. 464 043, 27 March 2017

TI No. 464 043 departs Roma Tiburtina with a Regional Trenitalia working. Being so numerous, this class of locomotive can be found in almost every part of Italy. The largest fleet is with Trenitalia.

TI No. 464 093, 29 March 2017

TI No. 464 093 departs from Roma Termini with a Trenitalia Regional working. The Class 464 locomotives are able to be worked as propelling locomotives with a driving trailer attached to the other end of the train. They are used by Trenitalia on short local workings, as well as on long-distance Regional services.

TI No. 464 095, 28 March 2017

TI No. 464 095 is seen arriving at Salerno with a Trenitalia Regional working. This was heading for Napoli Centrale, and the train consists of a rake of single-deck carriages. The Class 464 locomotives were built by Bombardier over a sixteen-year period.

TI 464 177, 13 October 2015

TI No. 464 177 is seen making a station call at Milano Rogoredo with a Regional working towards Milano Centrale. This view clearly shows the cover placed over the coupling on the majority of these locomotives to act as protection.

TI No. 464 186, 28 March 2017

TI No. 464 186 is seen waiting to depart from Salerno with a Regional service. The longer Regional trains in Italy, which are formed of Class 464 locomotives and carriages, sometimes have a loco at either end, working in multiple.

TI No. 464 223, 28 March 2017

TI No. 464 223 is seen departing from Salerno. This locomotive is on the rear of the train in the previous photograph, and is working in multiple with TI No. 464 186. Despite their short size, these locomotives still carry two pantographs, like most other traction in Italy.

TI No. 464 234, 28 March 2017

TI No. 464 234 is seen at Napoli Centrale while coupled to a rake of double-deck carriages. This view shows that the locomotive is missing the coupling cover. The locomotive is ready to depart as the rear pantograph is raised, rather than the front pantograph.

TN No. 464 237, 10 September 2014

TN No. 464 237 is seen at Chiasso in the attractive Trenord livery. Trenord have a sizeable fleet of Class 464 locomotives for use in the Lombardy Region around Milan. When in Chiasso the class have to be shunted by Swiss SBB locomotives as they only operate off the Italian 3,000 V DC electrics, whereas the wires in the yard are Swiss 15 kV AC.

TN 464 255, 13 October 2015

TN No. 464 255 is seen waiting to depart from Milano Centrale. This is another Class 464 locomotive operated by Trenord, and the loco is seen coupled to a rake of matching-liveried single-deck carriages.

TN 464 271, 2 August 2016

TN No. 464 271 is seen working through Milano Rogoredo with a Trenord passenger working. The Class 464 locomotives are used solely on passenger turns, and there are a handful in private use, with TPER owning ten locomotives and TFT owning just a single example.

TN No. 464 324, 13 October 2015

TN No. 464 324 stands at Milano Rogoredo while carrying a special Vivalto livery. This scheme was applied to a small group of Class 464 locomotives that were dedicated to working with coaching stock in the same livery. Today, TN No. 464 324 is operated by Trenord.

TI No. 464 340, 30 March 2017

TI No. 464 340 is seen propelling a rake of single-deck carriages into Livorno Centrale. This locomotive is based at Firenze, and is heading for Firenze Santa Maria Novella.

TI No. 464 359, 2 August 2016

TI No. 464 359 is seen looking respectable as it heads through the pretty station of Genova Nervi. This class of loco is the main workhorse of the Trenitalia Regional services. They also operate the Regionale Veloce services, which are the faster Regional trains.

TI 464 416, 30 March 2017

TI No. 464 416 is seen arriving at Livorno Centrale with a Trenitalia Regional working. This loco carries the new Regional livery of silver and blue, which improves the appearance of the locos greatly.

TI No. 464 450, 2 August 2016

TI No. 464 450 is seen on the left at Genova Brignole carrying Trenitalia livery, while on the right classmate TI No. 464 716 carries the new Regional livery. The two Class 464 locomotives sandwich shunter TI No. 245 2200, which is on station pilot duty.

TI No. 464 462 and TN No. 464 553, 13 October 2015

TI No. 464 462 and TN No. 464 553 are seen side by side at Milano Rogoredo. This view shows the difference in the liveries of the Trenitalia-operated locomotives and the Trenord-operated examples.

TI No. 464 464, 28 March 2017

TI No. 464 464 is seen at Roma Termini. This particular Class 464 locomotive carries a unique livery, complete with Quattro Sei Quattro branding applied to the front of the loco. A small number of the class were painted in Tilo livery for use around Milan, but all have now been repainted into Trenord livery.

TI No. 464 476, 30 March 2017

TI No. 464 476 is seen on the buffer stops at Firenze Santa Maria Novella. This station name is normally shortened to Firenze SMN. This train consists of a rake of double-deck Vivalto carriages, and they should match the new Regional-liveried Class 464s nicely when paired together.

TI No. 464 585 and TI No. 464 345, 31 March 2017

TI No. 464 585 and TI No. 464 345 are seen side by side at Firenze Santa Maria Novella. This view shows how different the new Regional livery carried by TI No. 464 585 is when compared to the traditional Trenitalia livery carried by TI No. 464 345.

TI No. 464 603, 1 August 2016

TI No. 464 603 is seen stabled at Torino Porta Nuova. This loco carries the new Regional livery, and is seen coupled to a rake of Trenitalia-liveried single-deck carriages.

TI No. 464 686, 29 March 2017

TI No. 464 686 stands on the buffer stops at Roma Termini. This was one of the last Class 464 locomotives to be delivered carrying Trenitalia livery, as from TI No. 464 689 onwards they were delivered carrying the new Regional livery.

TI No. 464 708, 28 March 2017

TI No. 464 708 stands at Formia-Gaeta, having arrived from Roma Termini with a Regional working. This view shows how well the train appears when the loco and coaching stock match in the new Regional colours.

TFT No. 464 880, 31 March 2017

TFT No. 464 880 is seen departing Arezzo. This is the only Class 464 locomotive in use with TFT (Transporto Ferroviario Toscano) and carries their livery. It is permanently coupled to the company's only rake of Vivalto carriages.

TI 470 004, 10 September 2014

TI No. 470 004 is seen departing Chiasso on the Swiss–Italian border with a working to Milano Centrale. At the time these units were used on the Milan to Zurich express workings. These services used to run under the Cisalpino banner, until the company and units were split between Swiss operator SBB and Italian operator Trenitalia.

TI No. 470 008, 30 March 2017

TI No. 470 008 arrives at Livorno Centrale with a Frecciabianca working. This Class ETR 470 nine-car unit was one of the former Cisalpino units that used to operate between Zurich and Milan, until they were replaced by the new Swiss Class 503 units.

NC No. 474 201, 10 September 2014

NC No. 474 201 is seen ready to depart from Chiasso yard in Switzerland with a rake of Cargowaggons, bound for Italy. This is the only Class E474/2 locomotive operating in Italy and at the time was operated by Nordcargo, but it now works for DB Cargo Italia.

OG No. 483 007, 13 October 2015

OG No. 483 007 is seen running through Treviglio with a rake of empty container flat wagons. This TRAXX locomotive is operated by Oceanogate, who in turn are owned by Contship, and they work container trains over Northern Italy.

NC No. 483 008, 2 August 2016

NC No. 483 008 passes through Milano Rogoredo with a rake of scrap wagons. This locomotive carries the standard TRAXX livery of green, but has had the grey replaced with blue and Nordcargo logos applied. Nordcargo locomotives now operate under the DB Cargo Italia branding, and NC No. 483 008 has brand-new TRAXX locomotive Akiem No. 483 224 in tow.

CTI No. 483 011, 2 August 2016

CTI No. 483 011 passes light engine through Milano Rogoredo. This is one of the busier stations in the Milan area for freight workings, and CTI No. 483 011 is operated by Captrain Italia.

OG No. 483 014, 13 October 2015

OG No. 483 014 passes through a wet Treviglio with a rake of Samskip containers. This locomotive carries one of the standard liveries for TRAXX locomotives on the Continent, and is the livery used by Belgian operator SNCB for its TRAXX locomotives.

XRI No. 483 017, 13 October 2015

XRI No. 483 017 is seen at a damp Milano Rogoredo with an Intermodal working. This locomotive is operated by Crossrail Italia and is unusual in that it has lost its 'E' prefix before its running number.

OG No. 483 018, 8 October 2014

OG No. 483 018 is seen at a busy Milano Rogoredo with a container working. This is one of the more striking liveries in use in Italy, being a very distinctive grey, red and pink.

NC No. 483 101, 8 October 2014

NC No. 483 101 passes through Milano Rogoredo with a rake of loaded trailer-rail wagons. Despite the Nordcargo branding, this locomotive is now operated by DB Cargo Italia.

DB No. 483 102, 13 October 2015

DB No. 483 102 is seen at a miserable Milano Rogoredo with a rake of scrap wagons. By this time this locomotive was operated by DB Cargo Italia, with Nordcargo's (the previous owner) branding removed. Despite this, the loco still retains its 'NC' on the front, as well as having DB logos.

NC No. 483 103, 10 September 2014

NC No. 483 103 prepares to depart from Chiasso yard with a rake of Cargowaggons bound for Italy. This locomotive is a member of the Bombardier-built TRAXX family of engines, and they are one of the main types of modern electric locomotives in use on the Continent.

NC No. 483 105, 2 August 2016

NC No. 483 105 passes through Milano Rogoredo, hauling a rake of brand new bogie tank wagons. At this time NC No. 483 105 was operated by Nordcargo, but it would soon be rebranded as DB Cargo Italia.

TI No. 485 014, 27 March 2017

TI No. 485 014 speeds through Roma Tiburtina with a Frecciabianca working. This unit is a Class ETR 485 unit, and there are fifteen of these nine-car units in operation, all on Frecciabianca workings. This unit carries the set number 44.

TI No. 506 022, 27 March 2017

TI No. 506 022 is seen departing Roma Tuscolana with a regional working from Fiumicino Aeroporto to Orte. There were ninety-nine of these four-car units built from 1998 onwards, with all except nine working for Trenitalia and the others working for Trenord.

TN No. 562 012, 13 October 2015

TN No. 562 012 arrives at Milano Rogoredo with a local Trenord working. This class of electric unit is known as Le 562, and this is one of sixty-eight driving trailers built from 1987 onwards by Ansaldo.

TN 582 011, 13 October 2015

TN No. 582 011 is seen at Treviglio while carrying Trenord livery. The Class Le 582 cars are the power cars that run with the Class Le 562 driving trailers, and they can run in sets of up to four carriages long.

TN No. 582 036, 13 October 2015

TN No. 582 036 is seen at Treviglio. This Le 582 car carried Trenitalia livery, but has Trenord logos applied, and also carries logos for Un Treno D'a Mare, which translates to 'A Sea Train'.

TI No. 600 107, 27 March 2017

TI No. 600 107 is seen departing Roma Tiburtina with a Frecciargento working, heading for Roma Termini. This Class ETR 600 unit was one of twelve built by Alstom Ferroviaria from 2006 onwards, and all are used on Frecciargento (silver arrow) workings.

TI No. 600 702, 27 March 2017

TI No. 600 702 arrives at Roma Tiburtina with a Frecciargento working. This set carries the number 2, and this car also carries the letter 'B', whereas the driving car at the other end carries the letter 'A'.

TFT No. 624 012, 31 March 2017

TFT No. 624 012 is seen stabled at Arezzo. This Class EBz 624 power car dates from 1932 and was rebuilt by FERVET in 1983. It is currently operated by TFT (Transporto Ferroviario Toscano) and is one of only two cars in use. The other car, TFT No. 624 009, is coupled to the other end of the five-car train.

FS No. 633 008, 12 November 2001

FS No. 633 008 is seen stabled at Modane while carrying original FS livery. There were nearly 150 of these locomotives built, both to Class 632 passenger and Class 633 freight designs.

TI No. 633 204, 8 October 2014

TI No. 633 204 passes through Milano Rogoredo while hauling TI No. 656 570. TI No. 633 204 still carries the old version of FS livery, despite Trenitalia being fourteen years old at the time.

TI No. 633 211, 2 August 2016

TI No. 633 211 is seen at Genova Brignole with a container working. The Class 633/2 locomotives were also equipped with multiple working equipment, and a start has been made on withdrawing the class from service.

TI No. 642 031, 30 March 2017

TI No. 642 031 is seen approaching a sunny Livorno Centrale with a local working. The Class ALe 642 cars work either in multiple with other Class 642 power cars or with Class Le 682 driving trailers.

TI No. 646 118, 29 March 2017

TI No. 646 118 stands condemned in the yard at Ancona. Nearly 200 of this class of locomotive were built from 1958 onwards by various builders, and all have today been withdrawn from service. They were used on both passenger and freight services.

TI No. 652 001, 10 September 2014

TI No. 652 001 stands in the yard at Chiasso, waiting to depart towards Italy with a freight working. This class of locomotive is a derivative of the Class 633 locomotives.

TI No. 652 002, 13 October 2015

TI No. 652 002 passes through Treviglio with a rake of scrap wagons. The similarity between this class and the Class 633 locomotives is very apparent.

TI No. 652 003, 8 October 2014

TI No. 652 003 passes through Milano Rogoredo with a rake of bogie tank wagons. This locomotive still carries the old FS livery, and is one of over 170 locomotives built by Ansaldo from 1990 onwards.

FS No. 652 034, 12 November 2001

FS No. 652 034 is seen stabled at Modane, on the Italian–French border, while still carrying FS livery. Trenitalia had only been operating for just over one year, and its livery was slow to be applied to its locomotives.

TI No. 652 065, 8 October 2014

TI No. 652 065 runs through Milano Rogoredo with a rake of LPG bogie tank wagons. This locomotive shows signs of the state some of the Italian locos run in, having suffered graffiti attacks.

TI No. 652 095, 30 March 2017

TI No. 652 095 is seen at Livorno Centrale with a single twin wagon containing just one liquid container. This wagon was suffering from severe wheel flats, and the train could only manage 10 mph as it passed through the station.

MIR No. 652 120, 30 March 2017

MIR No. 652 120 is seen calling at Livorno Centrale for a crew change. This loco has had its UIC code changed to Mercitalia from Trenitalia.

TI 652 133, 31 March 2017

TI No. 652 133 arrives at Terni with a rake of loaded scrap steel wagons. The loco was working top and tail with classmate TI No. 652 028, which was detached while the train was in the station.

MIR No. 652 156, 27 March 2017

MIR No. 652 156 is seen slowing for a signal check at Settebagni while hauling a rake of Cargowaggons. This is another loco to have had its UIC code changed to MIR, Mercitalia, from TI, Trenitalia.

TI No. 655 206, 13 October 2015

TI No. 655 206 is seen passing through a wet Treviglio with a mixed freight working. Included in the formation is a newly overhauled sleeper carriage.

TI No. 655 425, 29 March 2017

TI No. 655 425 is seen stabled at Foligno station. This view shows the unusual Bo-Bo-Bo wheel arrangement that many of the Italian locomotives run on. Over 500 of these unusual locomotives were built from 1975 onwards.

TI No. 655 475, 8 October 2014

TI No. 655 475 is seen passing through Milano Certosa with a rake of empty container flat wagons. The Class 655 locomotives differed from the Class 656s in that they are for freight use, have a lower top speed, and have different gear ratios.

TI 655 509, 13 October 2015

TI No. 655 509 is seen passing through Treviglio with a loaded container working. This class of loco is equally at home on passenger workings as on freight turns.

TI No. 655 513, 30 March 2017

TI No. 655 513 is seen stabled at Livorno Centrale. This loco is another that shows signs of having suffered a graffiti attack, which certainly affects most of the railways in Italy.

TI No. 655 519, 8 October 2014

TI No. 655 519 is seen at Milano Rogoredo with a rake of empty container flat wagons. This class of locomotives is very unusual in the fact that they are articulated, which is a very uncommon design.

FS No. 656 001, 27 March 2017

FS No. 656 001 passes through Roma Tiburtina, hauling electric locomotive FS No. 428 202. FS No. 656 001 was the original member of this class of locomotives that numbered over 500 engines. As such it has been retained as a historic locomotive and has been repainted back into its original FS livery.

TI No. 656 040, 13 October 2015

TI No. 656 040 is seen waiting to depart from Milano Centrale with a passenger working. The stock for this service comprised Austrian OBB single-deck carriages.

TI No. 656 082 and TI No. 656 431, 10 September 2014

TI No. 656 082 and TI No. 656 431 are seen waiting to depart from Chiasso, on the Swiss–Italian border, with a rake of four Swiss SBB carriages. This working was heading for Milano Centrale, and note how the second locomotive, TI No. 656 431, was being hauled dead.

TI No. 656 431, 10 September 2014

TI No. 656 431 is seen at Chiasso, backing onto a rake of Swiss carriages. When attached, this loco would be hauled dead towards Milano Centrale by classmate TI No. 656 040. A large number of these distinctive locomotives are now being taken out of service.

TI No. 656 570, 8 October 2014

TI No. 656 570 is seen being hauled dead through Milano Rogoredo by locomotive TI No. 633 204. This loco carries tail lamps, rather than having its marker lights illuminated. It also carries Liguria region markings above the Trenitalia logos.

TI No. 663 1129, 28 March 2017

TI No. 663 1129 is seen arriving at Salerno, running as just a single-car unit. These modern-looking units are in fact over thirty years old, and are used mainly on lightly loaded local workings. Most were built by Savigliano from 1983 onwards.

TI No. 663 1152, 28 March 2017

TI No. 663 1152 is seen stabled at Napoli Centrale. These units carry end-connecting doors to allow more than one unit to be coupled to another. Also of note are the impressive-looking deflector plates underneath the buffers.

EAV No. 668 113, 28 March 2017

EAV No. 668 113 rests on the buffer stops at Napoli Centrale. This single-car unit was from a family of units that totalled nearly 800 single-car sets, and is from one of the earliest batches produced. It was renumbered from ALn No. 668 1442 when it was purchased from the FS fleet.

EAV No. 668 118, 28 March 2017

EAV No. 668 118 is seen at Napoli Centrale. This view shows the gangway connector fitted to this end of the car. EAV No. 668 118 was formerly in the main FS fleet, numbered ALn No. 668 1472, and is one of just four similar cars used in the EAV (Ente Autonomo Volturno) fleet.

TI No. 668 1855, 28 March 2017

TI No. 668 1855 is seen stabled outside the shed building at Salerno. This single-car unit is from a batch of eighty-five built by Fiat Ferroviaria from 1971 onwards. Most of this batch is still in service today.

TI No. 668 3196, 31 March 2017

TI No. 668 3196 is seen stabled for the night at Pisa Centrale. The Class ALn 668 units are able to operate in multiple with their newer Class ALn 663 counterparts, and also have gangway connecting doors to allow passage between coupled units.

TN No. 711 001, 8 October 2014

TN No. 711 001 is seen arriving at Milano Certosa. This particular class of EMU was built by AnsaldoBreda and is used by Trenord, who are based in the Lombardy Region around Milan, on local suburban services. No. 711 001 carries LeNORD livery.

TN No. 711 032, 8 October 2014

TN No. 711 032 is seen arriving at Milano Certosa carrying full Trenord livery. These units can operate in anything from three to six-car formations. These units are also known at TSR (Treno Servizio Regionale) and are an updated version of the Class 426 and Class 506 TAF units.

TI No. 724 062, 28 March 2017

TI No. 724 062 is seen having arrived at Napoli Centrale. This Ale 724 class of EMU was built from 1982 onwards, and has started to be taken out of service, being replaced by Class ETR 425 Jazz units.

UM No. 776 017, 31 March 2017

UM No. 776 017 is seen stabled at Terni station. This class of single-car units is known as ALn 776. The units are operated by Umbria Mobilita and are used between Terni, L'Aquila and Sulmona. The external state of these units leaves a lot to be desired.

UM 776 072, 31 March 2017

UM No. 776 072 is seen at Terni. This single-car unit shows signs of being painted in a livery similar to the Trenitalia Regional livery, but this has been obliterated by graffiti vandals. These units were built by Fiat from 1985 onwards and like the Trenitalia Class ALn 663 units they have gangway connecting doors to allow them to operate in multiple.

TI No. D345 1021, 29 March 2017

TI No. D345 1021 is seen stabled at Orte. The Class D345 diesel locomotives were built by Fiat from 1970 onwards, with a total of nearly 150 being built, but today only around half of that number are left in use. No. D345 1021 carries the same attractive green and brown livery it carried when it was first introduced.

TI No. D445 1068, 30 March 2017

TI No. D445 1068 is seen at Siena, waiting to depart for Firenze Santa Maria Novella. This is the Italian big diesel class that is used on passenger workings in small pockets across the country. From 1974, 150 of these locos were built by Fiat.

TI No. D445 1122, 30 March 2017

TI No. D445 1122 is seen having arrived at Siena with a passenger working from Firenze Santa Maria Novella. This class of diesel locomotives now carries UIC numbers, with No. D445 1122 carrying the number 92 83 2445 122-0.

TFT No. ETT 22, 31 March 2017

TFT No. ETT 22 is seen arriving at Arezzo. There are just four of these Class ALn 501 units in service with TFT (Transporto Ferroviario Toscarno), and they are again identical to the Trenitalia ALn 501 Minuetto units.

TFT No. ETT 23, 31 March 2017

TFT No. ETT 23 is seen stabled at Arezzo station. These four units are known as the Elfo units by TFT. Of note is that the centre car of No. ETT 23 carries an overall advert.

DPO No. G2000 16, 1 August 2016

DPO No. G2000 16 is seen stabled just outside Torino Porta Nuova station. This diesel locomotive is used as a rescue engine, and is one of around fifteen that can be found dotted all around the Trenitalia network. Of note is the Class 464 adaptor coupling fitted to assist in rescuing those locomotives. These locomotives were built by Vossloh, and this one is operated by DP Dinazzano Po. Reggio Emilia.

TI No. MD 043, 27 March 2017

TI No. MD 043 arrives at Roma Tiburtina with a Regional working. These units are known as Class ALn 501s, and are from the Coradia family of units built by Alstom. There are 104 three-car diesel units in service, each carrying running numbers that start with 'MD'.

TI No. ME 066, 28 March 2017

TI No. ME 066 is seen at Salerno carrying Regional livery. The ME class of units are electric versions of the ALn 501 units, and are designated as Class ALe 501. Confusingly, No. MD01 carries the exact same individual car numbers as No. ME01, and this is repeated for the entire class.

TI No. ME 070, 28 March 2017

TI No. ME 070 is seen departing Salerno. When first introduced, a small batch of ALe 501 units replaced Class 464 locomotives on the Leonardo Express workings from Fiumicino Aeroporto to Roma Termini. No. ME 070 was one such unit. The Class 464s have since been replaced by brand-new Class ETR 425 Jazz units.

TI No. ME 093, 29 March 2017

TI No. ME 093 is seen arriving at Ancona with a Regional working. The family resemblance between these units and the Trenord ETR 245 units used on the Malpensa Express services, as well as the ETR 425 Jazz units, is immediately apparent. This family of units is also known as the Minuetto units.

GTT No. TTR 010, 1 August 2016

GTT No. TTR 010 is seen arriving at Torino Lingotto. This three-car unit is
Coradia units, and is identical to the Trenitalia Class ALe 501 units, also known a
these units in use with GTT (Gruppo Torinese Transporti) for local workings aro